MW01069525

# Spotlight on™ Social Skills, Ac
# Nonverbal Language

## by Carolyn LoGiudice & Paul F. Johnson

| Skills | Ages |
|---|---|
| ■ understanding and using appropriate nonverbal language | ■ 11 and up |
| ■ interpreting nonverbal signals re: emotions | **Grades** |
| ■ role-playing nonverbal communication | ■ 6 and up |

## Evidence-Based Practice

■ Children with limited language skills experience a poor quality of social interactions (Hadley & Rice, 1991; Fujiki et al., 1997; Craig, 1993; Cohen et al., 1998). Such children have greater deficits in social cognitive processing than children with typically developing language. They have particular deficits in identifying the feelings of each participant in a conflict, identifying and evaluating strategies to overcome obstacles, and knowing when a conflict is resolved (Cohen et al., 1998).

■ Social skills intervention can improve children's social cognitive skills (Timler et al., 2005).

■ Targeted language intervention with at-risk students may result in more cautionary, socially acceptable behaviors (Moore-Brown et al., 2002). Intervention for adolescents with language impairments may include objectives aimed at improving deficient social communication skills (Henry et al., 1995; Bliss, 1992).

■ For students with ASD, explicit instructions to attend to facial expression and tone of voice can elicit increased activity in the medial prefrontal cortex, part of the key network for understanding others' intentions (Wang et al., 2007).

■ Only 7% of the information we communicate to others depends upon the words we say; 93% depends on nonverbal communication (Mehrabian, 1971).

■ In selecting remediation targets within social communication among adolescents, clinicians should consider the relative importance of various communication skills in terms of enhancing peer communication. Communication skills involving social perspective taking (including nonverbal language) that focus on another person are more valued by adolescents than skills that focus on the speaker's thoughts or linguistics (Henry et al., 1995).

*Spotlight on Social Skills, Adolescent Nonverbal Language* incorporates these principles and is also based on expert professional practice.

## LinguiSystems

LinguiSystems, Inc.
3100 4th Avenue
East Moline, IL 61244

FAX:    800-577-4555
Phone:  800-776-4332
Email:  service@linguisystems.com
Web:    linguisystems.com

Printed in the U.S.A.
ISBN 978-0-7606-0780-0

# About the Authors

**Carolyn LoGiudice**, M.S., CCC-SLP, and **Paul F. Johnson**, B.A., are editors and writers for LinguiSystems. They have collaborated to develop several publications, including *Story Comprehension To Go, No-Glamour Sequencing Cards* and *Spotlight on Reading & Listening Comprehension.* Carolyn and Paul share a special interest in boosting students' language, critical thinking, and academic skills.

In their spare time, Carolyn and Paul enjoy their families, music, gourmet cooking, and reading. Carolyn is learning to craft greeting cards and spoil grandchildren. Paul, a proud father of three children, also enjoys bicycling, playing music and spending rare moments alone with his wife, Kenya.

# Table of Contents

# Introduction

Adolescents who have not acquired appropriate social skills on their own are unlikely to develop those skills without specific instruction. Activities in *Spotlight on Social Skills, Adolescent* include explicit teaching, modeling, observation, discussion, role-playing, and other guided practice to spotlight specific social skill areas from different perspectives in the context of everyday situations. These activities can be presented to individual students or small groups of students with similar skill deficits.

Before beginning any social skill training, you should evaluate each student's current performance. Determine whether the student has a performance deficit (has the skills but doesn't use them) or an acquisition deficit (lacks the skills or the discrimination of which behaviors to use in specific situations). The activities in this series are designed for students who need direct instruction and guided practice to acquire and master specific skills. Use the Pretest/Posttest, observation, teacher reports, and/or personal interview to select appropriate lessons to present. These are the books in *Spotlight on Social Skills, Adolescent:*

- Nonverbal Language
- Making Social Inferences
- Emotions
- Conversations
- Getting Along
- Interpersonal Negotiation

Since peer relationships are the most important to the majority of adolescents, this training resource contains content mostly targeted to adolescent concerns and peer relationships. Each activity sheet affords a chance to highlight a specific skill and to facilitate discussing that skill with your students. The more you personalize the activities with examples from the students' particular situations, the more effective your training will be.

*Spotlight on Social Skills, Adolescent: Nonverbal Language* unlocks the code of nonverbal behaviors that help us infer how someone feels and predict what the person might do next. As you present the activities, teach your students to become keen observers of others, especially their peers. How do they look when they greet each other? How do they act? What is interesting to them? How do they have conversations? What do they show with their faces? How do they move their eyes and why? What do they do with their hands and their bodies during a conversation? You might need to give your students specific things to look for at a time until they become effective observers. Keep talking with them about what they notice, guiding them to understand why their peers act the way they do.

Here are some ways to enrich your social skills training for nonverbal language:

- Frequently assess individual students and modify your training accordingly. Gather baseline data on specific behaviors, such as the number of times a student initiates a conversation or uses good nonverbal language to express a thought.

- Provide specific feedback and guidance as often as possible when doing the activities in this training series. Emphasize the positive and boost students' self-esteem by showing them they can control many of their social interactions with others.

- Have mirrors available for students to imitate nonverbal behaviors themselves. The more they try these behaviors, the more likely they will use them spontaneously in other contexts.

- Play muted snippets of movies or TV dramas. Frequently stop the action to ask what is going on and what nonverbal cues helped to make that clear. Then replay the same snippet with the sound on. Ask your students if the dialog has changed their impressions of what is going on.

- Videotape your students doing and discussing some of the activities, especially the role-playing tasks. Talk individually with your students about their performance, spotlighting what each student did well vs. what was inept or inappropriate. Have your students repeatedly watch taped segments in which they performed well to provide personal social scripts students can then apply in similar situations.

- Some nonverbal factors are not directly addressed within this book, yet these factors can convey important information. Look for teachable moments to incorporate modeling and discussion of these factors:

      Voice volume, tone, pitch, and quality
      Speaking rate and style
      Laughter
      Repairing errors as a speaker
      Personal appearance (grooming and dress)

- Present pictures from various sources and ask your students to detect nonverbal cues. Encourage your students to verbalize how such cues help us to make inferences about what someone is thinking or might do.

- Have your students play Pantomime, acting out statements or emotions. As your students become more skilled, encourage them to write their own items for peers to pantomime in a game context.

- Use the cards and activities in the *Nonverbal Language Kit* (LinguiSystems, 2003) to help your students identify and use key nonverbal behaviors.

- Use caution in encouraging students to increase or change their eye contact habits. Eye movements are largely unconscious and existing patterns may be resistant to change. Also, some students cannot process visual and auditory information at the same time with efficiency. Such students may need to avoid eye contact in order to get the meaning of what a speaker says, even if that means these students will miss the nonverbal cues from the speaker.

We hope you and your students enjoy *Spotlight on Social Skills, Adolescent: Nonverbal Language!*

Carolyn and Paul

5

## Pretest/Posttest

1. What is nonverbal language?

   _____

2. How do you know when you are standing too close to someone?

   _____

Without saying anything, demonstrate each emotion.

3. sadness          5. fear          7. disgust

4. surprise         6. anger         8. distrust

Use nonverbal language to communicate each message without talking.

9. What did you say?          12. That's a crazy idea!

10. That's fine with me.       13. Don't come any closer!

11. I'm very sleepy.           14. I don't believe you.

List four ways you can tell that someone is ready to listen to you.

15. _____

16. _____

17. _____

18. _____

# What Is Language?

Language is a system people use to share their thoughts, their ideas or their feelings with each other. People use language when they talk to each other. People also use language when they write or read.

Check each word in this list that uses language. Then talk with a partner about how each item you each checked involves language.

☐ 1. secret

☐ 2. list

☐ 3. photograph

☐ 4. story

☐ 5. phone book

☐ 6. TV ad

☐ 7. computer

☐ 8. fishing pole

☐ 9. calendar

☐ 10. diary

☐ 11. invitation

☐ 12. sandals

☐ 13. piano

☐ 14. map

☐ 15. conversation

☐ 16. dictionary

☐ 17. magnet

☐ 18. argument

☐ 19. book report

☐ 20. directions

☐ 21. gift

☐ 22. phone call

☐ 23. sandwich

☐ 24. newspaper

# What Is Nonverbal Language?

Nonverbal language is communication beyond a speaker's words. Nonverbal language adds expression and meaning to what we say with words.

When someone talks to you, the person's nonverbal language tells you much more than the words the person says. Think about these questions.

- What emotion does the person show?
- What do you notice about the person's eyes, nose and mouth?
- What is the person's posture?
- How loud is the person's voice?
- How close is the speaker to you?
- What gestures does the person use?
- Do the person's words match the person's nonverbal language?
- Does the person seem interested in talking with you?
- Does the person pay attention when you take a turn talking?

Try this for fun. Say the sentence "You think that I didn't do it" with as many different meanings as you can. You can use your body posture, your hands, your face, and your voice to send this message with different meanings. Write each different meaning you communicate for this sentence.

1. _____

2. _____

3. _____

4. _____

5. _____

6. _____

# Identifying Nonverbal Language ❶

Nonverbal language is communication besides the actual words we use. Check each item that sends a nonverbal message.

☐ 1. winking

☐ 2. resting your head on your hands

☐ 3. sleeping

☐ 4. pointing

☐ 5. nodding your head

☐ 6. brushing your teeth

☐ 7. raising your eyebrows

☐ 8. smiling

☐ 9. turning your back on someone

☐ 10. frowning

☐ 11. wearing glasses

☐ 12. shrugging your shoulders

☐ 13. waving

☐ 14. clapping

☐ 15. giving someone a "high five"

☐ 16. shaking your fist

☐ 17. pressing your lips firmly together

☐ 18. taking a picture

☐ 19. crossing your arms

☐ 20. coughing

☐ 21. pinching your nose closed

☐ 22. writing a note

☐ 23. sticking your tongue out

☐ 24. sighing

☐ 25. opening a book

☐ 26. tapping someone on the shoulder

☐ 27. drinking with a straw

☐ 28. tripping over something

☐ 29. crossing your fingers

☐ 30. looking at someone from the sides of your eyes

# Identifying Nonverbal Language ❷

Watch a half-hour TV show with characters who talk to each other. List as many ways as you can that the characters use nonverbal language.

1. _____

2. _____

3. _____

4. _____

5. _____

6. _____

7. _____

8. _____

9. _____

10. _____

11. _____

12. _____

# Personal Space

People have different ideas about how close to stand to talk with someone. You have to look for clues to know when you are too close or too far away from someone else for that person's comfort. You also need to let people know when they get too close to you.

Here is how most people in the U.S. think of the space around them:

| Distance | Kind of Space | How We Use It |
| --- | --- | --- |
| up to 1½ feet | intimate space | for very close friends or family |
| 1½ to 4 feet | personal space | for friends, classmates; for standing in line; for conversations |
| 4 to 12 feet | social space | for more formal social situations, such as talking to a sales clerk or the school secretary |

Here are some tips about using personal space so you don't bother people:

- Unless you feel very close to someone emotionally, don't stand closer to the person than the distance between your arm and your shoulder. Stand an arm's length away from the person.

- If someone backs off or turns away from you, you have come too close to the person. Backing away is a nonverbal signal for "I need more personal space between you and me."

- Don't touch other people unless you are very close to them emotionally.

1. Have a string or a tape measure handy. Ask a classmate to move toward you slowly. Tell the person to stop when you are the least bit uncomfortable. Measure the distance between you and record it below. Repeat this exercise with four other people. Then write your own personal space by averaging what you recorded.

   _____   _____   _____   _____   _____   My personal space _____

2. Watch what happens when you approach a partner. What does the person do when you get too close for the person's comfort? Write the verbal behavior (words) and the nonverbal language you notice.

   _____

   _____

# Personal Space ❷

Look at each picture. Notice the space between the people. Then guess the relationship of the people in each picture. Are they a family, friends, close friends, or people who work together?

1.

relationship _____

2.

relationship _____

3.

relationship _____

4.

relationship _____

Why is it important to respect other people's comfort zones?

_____

_____

# Personal Space ❸

Use tape or chalk on the floor to make this diagram.

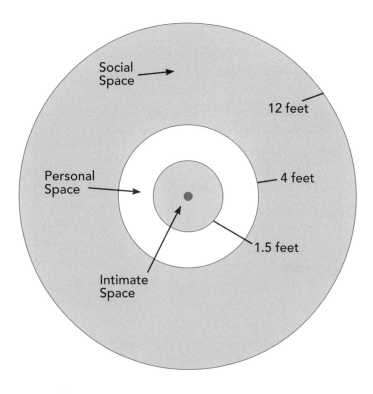

1. Stand in the center of the circles. Then ask someone to stand in the social space. Write the names of four people you would be comfortable having in your social space.

   _____     _____

   _____     _____

2. Next ask the person to move to the personal space zone. Write the names of four people you would be comfortable having in your personal space.

   _____     _____

   _____     _____

3. Then ask the person to move to the edge of your intimate space for a few seconds. Write the names of two people you would be comfortable having in your intimate space.

   _____     _____

# Posture ❶

Your posture is the way you hold your body.  Even if you don't mean to say anything by the way you position your body, your posture sends a message to other people.  It tells them what you think or how you feel.

Practice sending nonverbal messages with your posture.  Watch yourself in a mirror.  Match your posture to each of these descriptions.

1. You feel down.  You have no energy.  Drop your shoulders and lower your head forward.  Try not to look at anyone.  You don't want anyone to talk to you.

2. You are paying attention.  What you are hearing or seeing is very interesting to you.  Stand or sit up straight and look straight at what is so interesting to you.

3. You don't want the teacher to call on you.  You try to make yourself as small as you can.  Keep your head down.  Keep your arms close to your body.

4. You feel very relaxed and comfortable.  Make your muscles soft and relaxed.  Lean against something or sit or lie on the floor.  Look up to see if anyone wants to talk with you.  Make your face look calm or happy.

5. You want to seem very powerful and important.  Stand up straight.  Spread your legs and your arms apart to make yourself look bigger.  Take a deep breath and hold it to puff out your chest.  Keep all of your muscles tight.  You want to be ready to use your strength in an instant.

6. You are angry about something.  Cross your arms in front of you or put your hands on your hips.  Look straight ahead at the person or thing you are mad about.  Use your body energy to show your power.

7. You are proud of yourself because you just did something great.  Stand up and hold your head up high with pride.  Look around to smile at anyone who notices you.  Take a deep breath and puff your chest out.  Keep your chin up.

8. You are eager to see a friend.  You are "open" for a conversation.  Look straight ahead and keep your head level or slightly up.  Smile.  Relax your arms and hands; you can cross them or put them in your pockets, but keep them relaxed.

# Posture  

Look at these people's postures. Write what you guess each person is feeling or thinking.

1.

_____

_____

_____

2.

_____

_____

_____

3.

_____

_____

_____

4.

_____

_____

_____

# Gestures ❶

A gesture is a message you send with part of your body. A wave, a wink and a head shake are all gestures.

Some gestures replace words. For example, a wave can mean "Hi."

Write the letter of each gesture beside what the gesture means in words.

Photo courtesy of istockphoto.com © Luis Alvarez

| Meaning | Gesture |
|---|---|
| 1. ____ Please call on me. | A. arms straight up, hands in fists |
| 2. ____ Come here. | B. pinching your nostrils |
| 3. ____ I don't know. | C. pointing to something |
| 4. ____ Good for you! | D. raising your hand |
| 5. ____ Something stinks! | E. shrugging your shoulders |
| 6. ____ I'm sleepy. | F. cupping your hand behind your ear |
| 7. ____ I can't hear you. | G. holding your index finger to your lips |
| 8. ____ Don't do that. | H. pointing and wagging your finger |
| 9. ____ Yay, I won! | I. thumbs up |
| 10. ____ Be quiet. | J. beckoning with your finger |
| 11. ____ Look at that! | K. rubbing your eyes |

16

# Gestures ❷

Model using gestures to convey each message below. (There is often more than one way to gesture some of the messages.) Then cut these boxes apart. Give one at a time to a student. Help the student think how to enact the message by using a gesture. Ask the other students to guess the meaning of the gesture. Continue this activity until your students have mastered this list. Then work with them to generate other messages they could send with gestures.

| | | |
|---|---|---|
| That's okay with me. | Bravo! Good job! | Yes! I did it! |
| I have a headache. | Go that way. | I'm just kidding. |
| Good luck! | Oops! I messed up. | Congratulations! |
| I don't understand. | I have a great idea! | What time is it? |
| I know the answer! | I choose you. | That was bad. |
| Who me? | Back off. Stay away from me. | Wait, I'm thinking. |
| Call me. | I want three of them. | I don't want to hear it. |
| I'm warning you! | Give it to me. | Way to go! |
| Absolutely no way. | Yeah, sure. | Whatever, I don't care. |

# Gestures ❸

Many people use gestures as well as words to describe things.  Read each sentence.  Then say the sentence to someone.  Use gestures to add interest or information to the sentence.

1.  No, I don't want the big one.  I want the very little one.

2.  Just stop right there.

3.  Have you seen a girl with long, curly hair?

4.  We ordered the huge bucket of popcorn.

5.  Come on, let's shoot some baskets.

6.  This just doesn't make any sense at all.

7.  Spread just a little mustard on the bread.

8.  Carry this very carefully.

9.  That new house has huge windows.

10.  It's a great video game but it costs a lot of money.

11.  We hiked up over the mountain and down into the valley.

12.  We saw you coming when you were way over there.

13.  He is about five inches taller than I am.

14.  Oops, why didn't I think of that?

15.  Sure, come on over here.

16.  Call me tonight around 7:00.

17.  This sweater is too small and it makes me itch.

18.  I smelled something awful over here!

# Face Messages

We send many messages with our faces. The eyes, the eyebrows and the mouth are very important in showing how we feel about something.

Look in a mirror and imitate each face below. Make your eyes, eyebrows and mouth copy what you see. Think about how your face looks. Then write what feeling each face shows.

1.

_____

2.
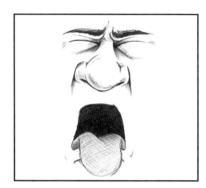

_____

3.

_____

4.

_____

5.

_____

6.

_____

# Face Messages ❷

As a warm-up activity, sit across from someone and take turns making faces. The other person should copy your face as closely as possible. Use a mirror if you need help making your facial expression look like your partner's expression. Talk about what feeling or message each expression might signal.

Then cut these boxes apart. Take turns drawing a feeling and making your face show that feeling to the rest of the group. Note that there may be more than one way to express a feeling and the same expression can show different feelings, depending on what the person is thinking.

| | | |
|---|---|---|
| admiration | anger | annoyance |
| begging | boredom | caution |
| curiosity | depression | disgust |
| disinterest | disrespect | enthusiasm |
| fatigue | fear | flirtation |
| friendliness | grief | helplessness |
| interest | jealousy | joy |
| pride | sadness | shame |
| shock | surprise | confusion |

# Interpreting Emotions ❶

Now that you know more about posture, gestures and facial expression, see how well you can tell what people might be thinking or feeling just from a picture. Write the letter of the description beside the picture it matches.

1. _____

2. _____

3. _____

4. _____

A. This person is angry. Body language shows the person doesn't like what's going on.

B. The person is excited about something and warning someone who is standing far away.

C. The person is happy and gesturing to say "good job."

D. The person is thinking hard.

# Interpreting Emotions ❷

Look at each picture carefully. Then write the emotion the person might be feeling. Describe the clues that suggest how the person feels. Then compare your impressions with someone else's ideas about these pictures.

1.

_____

_____

_____

2.

_____

_____

_____

3.

_____

_____

_____

4.

_____

_____

_____

# Interpreting Emotions ❸

Look at each picture carefully. Then write the emotion the person might be feeling. Describe the clues that suggest how the person feels. Then compare your impressions with someone else's ideas about these pictures.

1.

_____

_____

_____

2.

_____

_____

_____

3.

_____

_____

_____

4.

_____

_____

_____

23

# Interpreting Emotions ④

Look at each picture carefully. Then write the emotion the person might be feeling. Describe the clues that suggest how the person feels. Then compare your impressions with someone else's ideas about these pictures.

1.

_____

_____

_____

2.

_____

_____

_____

3.

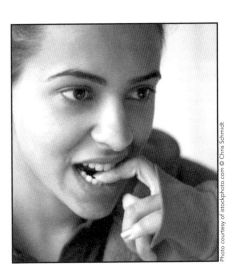

_____

_____

_____

4.

_____

_____

_____

# Interpreting Emotions ⑤

Look at each picture carefully. Then write the emotion the person or people might be feeling. Describe the clues that suggest how the person feels. Then compare your impressions with someone else's ideas about these pictures.

1.

_____

_____

_____

2.

_____

_____

_____

3.

_____

_____

_____

4.

_____

_____

_____

# Interpreting Emotions ⑥

Look at each picture carefully. Then write the emotion the person might be feeling. Describe the clues that suggest how the person feels. Then compare your impressions with someone else's ideas about these pictures.

1.

_____

_____

_____

2.

_____

_____

_____

3.

_____

_____

_____

4.

_____

_____

_____

# Interpreting Emotions ❼

Look at each picture carefully. Then write the emotion the person or people might be feeling. Describe the clues that suggest how the person feels. Then compare your impressions with someone else's ideas about these pictures.

1.

_____

_____

_____

2.

_____

_____

_____

3.

_____

_____

_____

4.

_____

_____

_____

# Ready to Listen ❶

We can tell by looking at someone if the person seems ready to listen to us.

- The person will have a neutral or happy facial expression.
- The person will look at you.
- The person will not be busy talking, working, thinking, or doing something else.
- The person will not look angry, excited or depressed.

Check the correct box below each picture to tell if the person is ready or not ready to listen to you.

1.

☑ ready
☐ not ready

2.

☐ ready
☑ not ready

3.

☐ ready
☐ not ready

4.

☐ ready
☐ not ready

# Ready to Listen ❷

We can tell by looking at someone if the person seems ready to listen to us.

- The person will have a neutral or happy facial expression.
- The person will look at you.
- The person will not be busy talking, working, thinking, or doing something else.
- The person will not look angry, excited or depressed.

Check the correct box below each picture to tell if the person is ready or not ready to listen to you.

1.
☐ ready
☐ not ready

2.
☐ ready
☐ not ready

3.
☐ ready
☐ not ready

4.
☐ ready
☐ not ready

5.
☐ ready
☐ not ready

6.
☐ ready
☐ not ready

# Joining a Group ❶

There are rules about when it's okay or not okay to try to join a group of people.

- Approach or stand by the group quietly.  Don't just barge in.
- If the group is busy doing something, walk away.  Wait for a better time to talk to them.
- Watch to see if anyone in the group looks at you.  If someone looks at you briefly and then looks back at the group, that means "not now."  If someone smiles at you or gestures for you to join the group, move into the group.
- Don't interrupt anyone in the group.  Wait until there is a pause or someone talks directly to you.

Look at each group.  Check open if the group looks ready for you to join them.  Check closed if the group doesn't look ready for you to join them.

1.

☐ open
☐ closed

2.

☐ open
☐ closed

3.

☐ open
☐ closed

4.

☐ open
☐ closed

# Joining a Group ❷

Look at each group. Check open if the group looks ready for you to join them. Check closed if the group doesn't look ready for you to join them.

1.

☐ open
☐ closed

2.

☐ open
☐ closed

3.

☐ open
☐ closed

4.

☐ open
☐ closed

5.

☐ open
☐ closed

6.

☐ open
☐ closed

# Active Listening ❶

When someone is talking to you, you should show that you are paying attention. These are good ways to show you are paying attention.

- Turn your body to face the speaker.

- Look at the person now and then, but don't stare.

- Nod your head sometimes to say "I understand" or "I agree" without using any words. You can also say "Mm-hmm" to let the person know you understand or agree with what the person is saying.

- If you don't hear or understand something, let the person know. Ask a question or make a face that shows you didn't get what the person said.

- Wait until the person signals you with eye contact or a pause to take a turn in the conversation.

These are bad habits for listening to others during conversations.

- Don't look at the person talking.

- Stare at the person.

- Keep moving parts of your body. For example, play with your hair, bounce your foot or fiddle around with your fingers.

- Interrupt the person.

Write three tips for yourself to remember to be a good listener in a conversation.

1. _____

   _____

2. _____

   _____

3. _____

   _____

# Active Listening

To practice showing good listening behavior during a conversation, follow these steps.

1. Find a conversation partner.

2. Write at least two ways you will show your partner you are listening while your partner takes a conversation turn.

   _____

   _____

   _____

3. Agree on a conversation topic with your partner.  You may choose from this list or think of your own topic.

   | | |
   | --- | --- |
   | a school activity | music you enjoy |
   | a class or teacher in your school | your plans for next weekend |
   | your hobby | a school rule you don't like |
   | a movie or TV show | the best field trip ever |

   topic _____

Have your conversation.  Try to take conversation turns for at least one minute.  Then rate your listening behavior below.  Give yourself a score of 2 (excellent), 1 (good) or 0 (poor) for each behavior.

_____ I faced the speaker.

_____ I looked at the speaker, but I didn't stare.

_____ I didn't interrupt the speaker.

_____ I nodded my head or said "Mm-hmm" to show I understood the speaker.

_____ I didn't make any distracting movements.  I kept myself still.

_____ I asked a question or made a questioning face if I didn't understand something.

Rating:  0-4 poor, 5-9 good, 10-12 excellent

# Tone of Voice

The tone of your voice makes a big difference in the messages you communicate to other people. It shows your emotions and how strongly you feel them.

*neutral tone*

*enthusiastic tone*

Your tone of voice can also change the whole meaning of what you say. Say each message to a partner. Emphasize the underlined word in each message. Ask the partner, "What did I mean?" after each way you say a message. If your partner didn't get the message you meant to send, try it again.

*sarcastic tone*

1. <u>That's</u> not my problem.  That's <u>not</u> my problem.  That's not <u>my</u> problem.

2. What do you <u>want</u>?  What <u>do</u> you want?  What do <u>you</u> want?

3. I thought you asked <u>me</u>.  I <u>thought</u> you asked me.  I thought you <u>asked</u> me.

4. Where are <u>you</u> going?  Where are you <u>going</u>?  <u>Where</u> are you going?

5. Please listen to <u>me</u>.  Please <u>listen</u> to me.  <u>Please</u> listen to me.

6. I'm <u>so</u> sorry you saw that.  I'm so sorry <u>you</u> saw that.  I'm so sorry you <u>saw</u> that.

7. <u>Your</u> shirt is fabulous.  Your shirt is <u>fabulous</u>.  Your <u>shirt</u> is fabulous.

8. What did you <u>eat</u>?  What <u>did</u> you eat?  What did <u>you</u> eat?

9. Next time just <u>ask</u> me.  <u>Next</u> time just ask me.  Next time just ask <u>me</u>.

# Tone of Voice

Practice using your tone of voice to make messages mean different things or show different emotions. Say each message at least three different ways to a partner. Ask the partner, "What did I mean?" after each way you try a message. If your partner didn't get the message you meant to send, try it again.

1. Tell me what you really mean.

2. Does anyone know what I'm talking about?

3. Tell me how I look now.

4. How long have you been practicing?

5. This time I'm telling you the truth.

6. I'm not the one who snitched on you.

7. I know why you sat next to her.

8. Tell me what you really mean by that.

9. If I were you, I wouldn't tell anyone what you did.

10. Maybe you already know the answer to that question.

11. Why would I be mad at you?

12. You're the only one who really knows me.

13. Why doesn't he just get the message?

14. Let me know when you're ready.

15. That is just what I wanted to happen.

16. Why don't you just ignore me?

# Role-Playing ❶

Cut these strips apart and put them into a box or bag. Have a student draw one strip and enact the message to a group of students. Ask the group to interpret the performer's emotions and message, based on observing the student's posture, gestures and facial expression. Allow the use of props where appropriate.

- - - - - - - - - - - - - - - - - - - - - - - - - - - - - - - - - - - - - - - - - - - - -

1. (Give this message without speaking.) This homework is really hard. I'm frustrated because I don't understand how to do it.

- - - - - - - - - - - - - - - - - - - - - - - - - - - - - - - - - - - - - - - - - - - - -

2. (Give this message without speaking.) I wonder if it's going to rain.

- - - - - - - - - - - - - - - - - - - - - - - - - - - - - - - - - - - - - - - - - - - - -

3. (Give this message without speaking.) Hi! If you want to talk to me, I'm ready to listen.

- - - - - - - - - - - - - - - - - - - - - - - - - - - - - - - - - - - - - - - - - - - - -

4. (Give this message without speaking.) How do you like my shirt?

- - - - - - - - - - - - - - - - - - - - - - - - - - - - - - - - - - - - - - - - - - - - -

5. (Give this message without speaking.) What time is it?

- - - - - - - - - - - - - - - - - - - - - - - - - - - - - - - - - - - - - - - - - - - - -

6. (Give this message without speaking). I want to know what the guy next to me is writing on his paper.

- - - - - - - - - - - - - - - - - - - - - - - - - - - - - - - - - - - - - - - - - - - - -

7. (Give this message without speaking.) It's sooo hot in here!

- - - - - - - - - - - - - - - - - - - - - - - - - - - - - - - - - - - - - - - - - - - - -

8. (Give this message without speaking.) Check out what someone is doing over there.

- - - - - - - - - - - - - - - - - - - - - - - - - - - - - - - - - - - - - - - - - - - - -

9. (Give this message without speaking.) Do you have a pair of scissors I could use?

- - - - - - - - - - - - - - - - - - - - - - - - - - - - - - - - - - - - - - - - - - - - -

10. (Give this message without speaking.) Would you like to come with me?

- - - - - - - - - - - - - - - - - - - - - - - - - - - - - - - - - - - - - - - - - - - - -

36

# Role-Playing ❷

Cut these strips apart and put them into a box or bag. Have a student draw one strip and enact the message to a group of students. Ask the group to interpret the performer's emotions and message, based on observing the student's posture, gestures and facial expression. Include interpreting tone of voice for situations involving speaking. Allow the use of props where appropriate.

---

1. (Give this message without speaking.) I'm starving. Do you have anything to eat?

---

2. (Give this message without speaking.) I can't find my wallet and I'm really worried about it.

---

3. (Give this message without speaking.) Just go away. Leave me alone.

---

4. You are overweight and you hate to exercise. Use good nonverbal language and tone of voice as you say, "I just love to exercise."

---

5. Your sister left a mess in the kitchen. Your parent tells you to clean up the mess. Use good nonverbal language and tone of voice as you ask, "Why can't she clean it up?"

---

6. You are trying to work and someone is making a loud noise. Use good nonverbal language and tone of voice as you say, "I can't work with all this noise!"

---

7. (Give this message without speaking.) Yes, I'm listening to you. I understand what you are saying.

---

8. (Give this message without speaking.) I'm very busy. Please don't bother me right now.

---

9. (Give this message without speaking.) I can't read what's written on the board.

---

10. (Give this message without speaking.) I'm trying to make you laugh.

---

# Role-Playing ❸

Cut these strips apart and put them into a box or bag. Have a student draw one strip and enact the message to a group of students. Ask the group to interpret the performer's emotions and message, based on observing the student's posture, gestures and facial expression. Include interpreting tone of voice for situations involving speaking. Allow the use of props where appropriate.

1. (Give this message without speaking.) Thanks for this great gift! I love it!

2. (Give this message without speaking.) Eeww, this lotion smells terrible!

3. You are terrified of snakes. You see a snake slither across the floor about five feet from you. Use good nonverbal language and tone of voice as you say, "A snake!"

4. Someone asks you to a party and you really want to go. Use good nonverbal language and tone of voice as you say, "Sure, I'll be there."

5. A friend tells you a joke and hopes you think it's a good one. Laugh as though you think the joke is great.

6. (Give this message without speaking.) I'm daydreaming about something that made me happy.

7. (Give this message without speaking.) I can't remember where I left my hat.

8. You are talking with your parent. You see a good friend walking toward you. Encourage your friend to come over to you and your parent.

9. You are listening to a friend talk. Without speaking, let your friend know you didn't understand what he just said.

10. You are shopping for new shoes. Use good nonverbal language and tone of voice as you tell the shoe clerk, "These just aren't my style."

# Role-Playing

Cut these strips apart and put them into a box or bag. Have a student draw one strip and enact the message to a group of students. Ask the group to interpret the performer's emotions and message, based on observing the student's posture, gestures and facial expression. Include interpreting tone of voice for situations involving speaking. Allow the use of props where appropriate.

1. (Give this message without speaking.) I'm really nervous about taking this test.

2. (Give this message without speaking.) I'm frustrated that my pen has run out of ink.

3. Your friend just won an important race. Use good nonverbal language and tone of voice as you say, "Way to go!"

4. Someone tries to stare you down, hoping to frighten you. Use good nonverbal language and tone of voice as you say, "I'm not impressed."

5. A classmate is standing too close to you as she talks to you. Without speaking, let her know you want more personal space while she's talking to you.

6. A friend is talking to you. You disagree with what your friend wants you to do. Without speaking, let your friend know that you disagree.

7. A friend offers you an apple or an orange for a snack. Without speaking, let your friend know that either snack is fine with you.

8. You are at the movies with a friend. Your friend keeps talking to you but you want to hear the movie. Without speaking, let your friend know what you want.

9. You are choosing a pastry at a coffee shop counter. Use good nonverbal language and tone of voice as you say, "Not that one, the first one in the row."

10. A friend grabbed your cell phone to tease you. Without speaking, tell your friend to give it back to you.

# Answer Key

Example answers are given for your reference. Accept other logical answers as correct.

**Page 6**
1. communication not based on words
2. The person moves away or acts uncomfortable.
3.-8. appropriate facial expression to match each emotion
9.-14. appropriate posture, gesture and facial expression to convey the message
15. The person looks neutral or happy.
16. The person looks at you.
17. The person is not busy.
18. The person is not angry or excited.

**Page 7**
Checked box for all except these:
3. photograph
8. fishing pole
12. sandals
13. piano
17. magnet
21. gift
23. sandwich

**Page 8**
Answers will vary.

**Page 9**
Checked box for all except these:
6. brushing your teeth
11. wearing glasses
18. taking a picture
20. coughing
22. writing a note
25. opening a book
27. drinking with a straw
28. tripping over something

**Pages 10-11**
Answers will vary.

**Page 12**
1. family
2. friends
3. students/coworkers
4. close friends

**Pages 13-14**
Answers will vary.

**Page 15**
1. angry, unimpressed, doubtful
2. tired, bored
3. happy, peaceful
4. bored, depressed

**Page 16**
1. D
2. J
3. E
4. I
5. B
6. K
7. F
8. H
9. A
10. G
11. C

**Pages 17-18**
Answers will vary.

**Page 19**
1. angry, mad
2. disgusted
3. afraid, frightened
4. happy
5. sad
6. surprised

**Page 20**
Answers will vary.

**Page 21**
1. B
2. D
3. C
4. A

**Page 22**
1. surprised, afraid; eyes open, fingers to mouth
2. depressed, bored; slumped, supporting head with hand/arm
3. stern; pointing at us, stern expression, eyebrows lowered
4. thrilled; smiling, arms up with loose fists

**Page 23**
1. happy, relaxed; smiling, casual posture
2. sad, thoughtful; looking down, hugging herself
3. surprised/frightened; eyes wide, eyebrows up, mouth open wide, holding hands to face
4. guarded, defensive; leaning back, shoulder raised, not smiling, staring at us

**Page 24**
1. bored, tired; resting head on chair, not smiling
2. angry; shouting at phone, eyes closed, brows frowning
3. worried, nervous; biting finger
4. surprised, shocked; mouth open, jaw dropped

**Page 25**
1. happiness; smiling, comfortable, close together
2. angry; staring at us, snarling nose/mouth with lots of teeth showing
3. sad, depressed; hugging self, looking down
4. puzzled, annoyed; frowning, upper lip pulled back

**Page 26**
1. shock; holding cheeks with hands, open eyes
2. disgusted; eyes squeezed shut, nose wrinkled, tongue out
3. surprised; eyes and mouth wide open
4. angry; yelling, frowning, hand raised for emphasis

**Page 27**
1. joy; smile, gift bag
2. fear; covering self, staring
3. sad, lonely; sad face/eyes
4. angry; facing away from each other, arms crossed

**Page 28**
1. ready
2. not ready
3. not ready
4. ready

**Page 29**
1. ready
2. not ready
3. not ready
4. ready
5. ready
4. not ready

**Page 30**
1. closed
2. closed
3. open
4. closed

**Page 31**
1. closed
2. closed
3. open
4. closed
5. open
6. open

**Pages 32-39**
Answers will vary.

19-10-987654

Copyright © 2008 LinguiSystems, Inc.